Wall to Wall Speaks

Princeton Series of Contemporary Poets
For other books in the Series, see page 108

DAVID MUS:
WALL TO WALL SPEAKS

PRINCETON UNIVERSITY PRESS

Copyright © 1988 by Princeton University Press
Published by Princeton University Press, 41 William Street,
Princeton, New Jersey 08540
In the United Kingdom: Princeton University Press, Guildford, Surrey

All Rights Reserved
Library of Congress Cataloging-in-Publication Data will be
found on the last printed page of this book

ISBN 0-691-06728-7 (alk. paper)
ISBN 0-691-01444-2 (pbk.)

Publication of this book has been aided by funds from the bequest
of Charles Lacy Lockert (1888-1974)

This book has been composed in Linotron Bodoni

Clothbound editions of Princeton University Press books
are printed on acid-free paper, and binding materials are
chosen for strength and durability. Paperbacks, although satisfactory
for personal collections, are not usually suitable for library rebinding

Printed in the United States of America by Princeton University Press,
Princeton, New Jersey

Cover illustration: Wash drawing by George Ball
Cover lettering by Stacy M. Wszola

ACKNOWLEDGMENTS

The following poems originally appeared in *Poetry*:

"Rain . . . ," Blake's Seasons, Four Last Poems,
Journey of the Magi, Wall, An Evening Walk . . . ,
Alfoxton Park, from "The Joy of Cooking," The Window,
Crust and Key, and December

The *Beloit Poetry Journal* originally published the following:

Nightingale, after Keats

CONTENTS

April Divinail   ix

From *The Joy Of Cooking*
   Recipe   3
   Cooked Goose   4
   Temperatures   5
   La Cuisine Française   6
   Conserves   7

"Rain . . ."   8

Blake's Seasons
   "To Spring"   15
   "To Summer"   16
   "To Autumn"   17
   "To Winter"   18
Nightingale, after Keats   19
Journey of the Magi   22
Four Last Poems   25

Wall   29
The Window   36

An Evening Walk, Some Years Later   44
Alfoxton Park   54
Crust and Key   60
December   68

Before the Hill
   Hillside   77
   The *Chevrefoil* of Marie de France   83
   Terrain   90
   Tree   103

APRIL DIVINAIL

The eyes released from school and going dutch
Revisit Leyden, Rotterdam, The Hague;
The brain puts on the old shows summer stock,
Reminds you in translation you're the plague,
Not its king, Venus' prey who lost his touch
With boar, Faust too keyed-up to pick the lock.

Leaf careened over snow, pitted olive,
Marble crushed and egg cracked into batter
Seem to intelligence definitive,
While piercing eyes perform their parodies
Limpid winter and summer winds batter
Subsisting grays mirroring paradise.

Solids slip away at the approach of sleep
Like the oars' handfuls of river
The tiny cyclones of precision and shape
Sliding among the quiet reeds
Or fall from the eyes like scales
And color leaving light

white unblemished illumining little
not in it spectacle rage the island
there is no such way of saying this thing

L'action n'est pas la vie
mais une façon de gâcher quelque force
un énervement.

the wooden spring recoils the window shade

what am I

from The Joy of Cooking

RECIPE

Take three days off from work and the driven car,
A stiff walk to the store to get tired some,
Two hours in a straight-chair the last evening,
Young fingers out of your hair, mouth or nose;

Combine with these simplest movements simpler,
Adding as whimsy suggests vertical strokes,
Folding in boldly trivial and obscene
Left-overs and forgetting nothing start again;

Compound the lark kite down wind's singing sky,
Enjoin the ripe poppy wheat, whole field mask,
The boxwood predicating pine-cone maze;

Rehearse yourself to no audience at all,
Reverse the very syllables till foreign,
Undress repeating each gesture motionless.

COOKED GOOSE

Splendid unearthed by some less ignoble
Juncture his servant's proximate mutism,
Each feature first confronted with the fact
Modeling its obduracy in depth
Shakes off impassible all knowledge of
The missing *collier* just now forever
Discovered, all traffic with such world as
Milord's stones, plate, heirloom invaluables
Denied, denied by the kidney-stiff lips,
Varicated moleskin cheeks, glassen eyes.

Grandfather's father's attic journals young
Had told in their own words he testified
How he died inside while upstairs like gods
They quaffed amber liquid and sesame,
The kitchen writhed, his hand turned furtive shone.

The yellowed light, my eyes choked with proud flesh,
This string of doubtful paste I sit fingering.

TEMPERATURES

The Shepherd's Pie takes its final browning.
He lived on pasturage I only guess,
Rock, lime, furze, great cliffs not like ships at sea
But the sea itself with ships upon it,
And its blind, helpless rush to its limits,
Lee shore and tempest sail, when distress or
The light effacing depth leaves innocence
("Innersense," had he said, "an innersense").
If I could see through the light, to its shoals,
Not a source but a haven, its image
Be focussed and observed here (this chamber
Dwelt in, the unchanging light, calming you
Like the dark passage from self-loathing to
Self-possession but with content inverse . . .)
The oven smokes, I fail, signally.

LA CUISINE FRANÇAISE

This mist had come in, in those few moments—
no, first I had come with Arthur, we were
ferried to Belle Isle and stood at the cliffs
looking west towards America on
the sea-dial, sun-strode, we the pivot when
this mist came in still bright as we turned from
bright sea, bright sun, in keeping not at all
with the things seen, sea and sky's clean corners;
and Sir Kay sent ahead came out speaking
without lips of the cook-book he had made
in Esperanto, "for they knew not our
northern ways," pointing to the faded sun
made of mist over his head, not this place
we gave our names to, not our path, our day,
our birth which we could not tell of outright.

CONSERVES

Season, ending, makes no sign, but the wind
And the light which rake across the vine change,
Fall away, bring the months to mind in chains
Of figures round its iron calender;
Rise and set of years sheds remembered light,
No other, while in this raw hour, outside,
A season writhes along the shaken vine,
Dies, and drags to its death some fruitless pride.

Fruit which comes away light from the main stalk,
Bearing no blemish, will last a winter
In still, cool places. Fruit which holds the stalk
May be cankered or green, do not force it,
Crude hands make a sour stomach. Fruit fallen
Will be bruised, though none show: it rots or stews.

There is no ideal time for canning.

"RAIN . . ."

I do set my bow in the cloud, and it shall be for a token of a covenant between me and the earth. —GENESIS 9:13

Rain.

Agate and coral ice your ripple brow,
Lurching into spray, shuddered loose from
Filed edges, an array of sparks, the wave struck
Quite into glaives, bristling milled marble's edge,

Positive sea of veined sides, froth caught,
Pearl cut from diamond, chased upright into a
Broach, watery weak, and sounded under strings,
Shell-white lacing foam with green deep stuff,

A knifing back of echoes, regular tune's
Refrain remembered, ready to beat as
The crystalline structures picked up from stone
Depths of sea, stone-stiff, beaten swells, been,

Pluck long jewels over beach before beach
Receive, resolve water and sand-sound,
Hard and something triumphant, whose trough, double-
Stopped, my silence rides seeing no wave but water.

Keep still to listen. Crash of wave betrays
Crash of wave ahead there, that beach part
Which receives, resolves, remembers, the fashion's
Brought up the wonder of old, well-turned talk:

"Contriving these jewels, bets before bet's
Been lost, wager marched off at the quick-step,
Heart where something triumphs, tough, where double-
Edged, my silence writhes seeking no way wider."

Still, again. No whisper, not a hint follows
The dummy lure as wave on wave blind
Like sheep to the beach, no humming ear takes up
Such praise, takes morbid praise for greeting.

Where is the listening post? That fresh trough,
Finger of air cut and trimmed by two waves,
Stuck in the ear? This mouth sees what the pearly
Inner-ear bone, blade-thin, might have spoken.

"But you *did* just speak to me where you stood
  High on that dune of sand, mute, off in some
  Perfect fit of love, since I rushed at you,
  Rain streaming from my face and features and

"Hit, made my point, arms almost as iron
  About your neck from behind, cheek frozen
  To a quartz ground into your cropped scalp,
  Bared the nape kept inside-warm and dry with scarfs,

"So that you turned, jarred, battered full circle,
  Thrown back to me by force which works, and grabbed
  Out finding me small as I'd be, though
  Mouth perished in my hair, tongue seeking my ear.

"You have no permission to ask. Should I
  Beg leave to overwhelm you? How could I not
  Hoist you from within, when you reply?"
"Your spite is not to see what I deny."

Brow beyond severe brow rise, silent,
Containing gaudiness as splashed with caught
Color, over a tumid hump of water,
The ceramic portrait of lucid gel,

Facets flood-lighted, swollen by gush from
Underneaths of liquid jade, erects
Plate-glass shape of gleam in depth, black-green
The glisten, body of white sweat, shoving out, on,

Plucking long jewels over beach before beach
Receive, resolve water and sand-sound,
Hard and something triumphant, whose trough, double-
Stopped, my mouth rides seeing no wave but water,

Bobs gagging at salt and bitter, noisy dreams how
Some impenitent flower of its strength,
The wave's cream, turns light, rainbowing bows,
Turns and falls like rain, like waterfall.

Blake's Seasons

From the English of Wm Blake (1783)

"TO SPRING"

My God! The morning buttonholed me and you,
Young Spring, slid down the facets from its crystal-
Linity; can you see us here, this earth mote,
Now it unites millions' faces turned for you?

The earth budges and peopled calls to itself,
And swells with us and our echoes towards your
Lucent enshrining; withdraw that consent just
Once, come smooth and sharp to stand within our voice!

Try rising with the sun as I have seen you
So our breath may catch at your warmth, lapped and tamed
In daily humbling; in dew and jewels embrace
The wintered soil still wincing from its last loss.

With your cherishing, deft hands, yourself, garnish
Her naked force, with your tongue luster her skin;
Then leave her flare with your bewildering flame,
Whose clear flesh was bounded to abound in you.

"TO SUMMER"

Whoosh and he's gone, passing you by and there's no
Stopping him: Hey, Summer, the errand can wait,
Too brilliant those skylights you cut in our calm,
Simmer down! So many times when you were not
So overworked we gazed through picture windows
At your brain, friends to its purple veining health;

At your flexed sinews oiled in the sun, your throat
Taut and humming, your swart firm buttocks in our
Back yard, the loaves and gut of your arm on Noon's.
If now you arrived and hurrying stripped to
Nude in our local wood, postured a second
The pelvis pushed forward in freedom and dove
Between our hills . . . Hidden! "Oh Summer, how proud!"

It is well known, ours is a land of culture.
Poets and lovers here can court heart to heart,
No southern fripperies; our honest youngsters
Hold their own dancing and singing with the best;
We too touch sticky leaves, burnt sky, water, light,
And poems to pierce the summer tedium.

"TO AUTUMN"

    Fresh from the slaughter rolling up, you, huge Autumn,
    The year done in and its guts dangled still wet-bright
    Over your back, while I hold it try, please, slipping
    Into one of my thinnest thoughts, braid on my force
    Your refined gaieties until with our gimp we
    Puppet the slain to life, sustain the victory:

"Our sap mounts, and tight roses shudder in their husks,
    Already the sun has lifted, heated the soil
    Unclothed out of mind: new bloomings twitched into shape
    Bury the day head to toe and Summer's head spins,
    Earth verticled, and heavy shaken by frenzy
    Fractures his image, crowds himself onto the floor:

"Here at home pet joys furnish a typical tree
    Now it's fruited, to pirate its meat round a seed,
    And I coursing work out leisure through the garden."
    Long as he could stand it, so he would speak with me,
    Gentle Autumn, rose relaxed it seemed and vanished
    Into a snow-flurry, left me to bear his guilt.

"TO WINTER"

"Keep in keep out, why should I expect self-
Knowledge from you, you barbarian, Winter?
Where and what you dug up in yourself is North,
For your steadiness of nerve there, keep still!"

No ears to plug mindless the brute his strength
Throws out with himself and consequence into
What welter, up and down flaying the unknown:
I keep my peace, and will not let him see.

But he has you, shivered you up with him
Into parchment and pemmican, splits the crust
Of your life, shuts up my mouth, cups our globe
Like an orange, peels it to the trembling loins.

Once let him clamber to his pride there's no
Cry, none, against his omniscience: you'll struggle
In a drowning throat till Heaven drops half way
And slams the vision back under Silence.

NIGHTINGALE, AFTER KEATS

August. Winter evening. I walk in.
To have left such sky, winter of it,
The sky. Inside, the eye reminisces.

Here's the match-stick. I call it: crocus.
Swelling alight, new breed, forced, kindling,
Word shattering visible. And ancient.

The hearth lights the room, I remember.
What to name what I heard. Is it the
Invisible impossible bird?
I reason backwards. Come so far, death
Inbreeding, new violence appearing,
Peremptory beauties and throughout
Such waking as an earlier man's
Dismay got at only deep in dream.
Though an artist in his reasoning way.

The cuckoo strains into the thick air,
The stupe. Dropping bald saccharine grains
Into the slow evening. Rolling his
Blindly saccharine pearl, again and
Again into the wash of evening,
Naming himself away. Something like:
The commonest sister's hand beading.
The oarsman forcing his stroke upstream.
The man trying for sleep and can't get it.

What to name what I hear. What stirring,
Dark wobble in the foliage,
Won't leave me and night alone. What if:
"You're always trying to make an ending,
As if dreading the putting out of mind
Much less than body's failing now, full pain,
Collapse of loosened beams, the choking dust,
Death the high calling you didn't follow,
Taking all pain short of that, counterstress
Made of me in such architecture, thus."
I won't sell for a song a hard-won
Lucidity. "You could make sense, it's done."
Behind the weave of craft, to whistle
In the dark. "Take it up with the highest
Ranges of speech, Alps of the vaulted word,
Iciest oracles, the final forms,
Nameless sounding shapes, Mt. Blanc, Matterhorn."

I go back. For not knowing I have
Quested the bird in April when all
The modern months were husked from mind.
Sun-motes Salome and the sun falls,
In the screen of brown thrush, browner wren,
Lark, tiny cross of vehemence,
Under the mud the toad keeping time,
Cuckoo, Embden geese or Gay's tractor
Stinking up the valley, there is, or
Was the dark warble, the extra voice.

Then in, in with a cry the bird
Lifted to high hope's ceiling sang and
Stuck, stood in starless skies whose night
Dashed questions to my window, in,
I'm into him and imagining
It, the night plumage beating in
My face and eyes, heart in mine
And the throat throb and thrush winged
Lift into empty sky up the night
Of night's vein, rift in its ore,
Over in one song heart without halt
Hell channel, dark continent and
Now the highest serpentine Alps,
The most frozen marbling Alps crossed
In night night yielding a burst of
Carnival, the sun, the warmth the
Glee, Italian end, dawn's Rome, the sun.

Cyclamens strung and coiled pinking
Viterbo's plowed outskirts that last
October morning. Here was my own
Precise calling in sight. And to have
Plucked it clear, sober from its sad
Aristotelian scene, fig and grape
Straining toward silent hand, docile
Wicker, sodden staves, ancient streaming tun.

Here. And months after. The name sticks.
The sky, cyclamen, opens. I've
Used up night, working it out, again:
"Have I ever heard the nightingale?"
From such terms, how know or cease. What
Do I stand for, what ignominies.
The windy hollow where the music
Fled proves what song caught better ears one
Dying spring. Made me Charles Brown
Say it to see what in the word sky
Stands. The month turns, without peace or
Ending is gone. In June the cuckoo
Hushes for summer, the singers are
Cut down to me, change to this, song to this one.

JOURNEY OF THE MAGI

1

At points we walked in walls of sugar-cane;
at others in olive groves, the bitter
      olive growths,
  on always the same white roads
        dust

                and the light mingled, penetrable.
Here was a limited space to be filled.

            At the end
           of the island a flat
           sky rises
           miming air
           which floods the hills, sea which
           crowns the hills.

           Our walking
           like the day
           kept ending as something
           else, is not
           walk where it is ended,

           the island no longer
           island, undergoing
           the sea, but shore.

2

Barely enough room for the day's walk.
I stop, half way, over the stream.

The stream: its surface, insistently penetrable,
        like a wall, to a fixed depth only;
        refusing to foil the gaze, continuing
        to be itself only, like the stream

              which refuses to stand up on its hind legs,
              for instance, and admit its near total
              lack of conviction, its extreme reserve.

Striding before me, the same blind mirage,
alive only in its refusal to quit or yield
entry; like a flat back-drop close up.

On these sands I build hope: of a flatness
        lording it over this impeded march,
        this progressive wrench, this forsaken motion,
        this statement aghast of feet through space.

A gentle rise.
Suggesting to be sure a new start,
        its end, as horizons horizon.

              I could turn back at the top
              remembering the city abandoned.

3

        The wood block, water-
        logged at last, come to rest;
        and not on the evasive beach,
        or, by an inner movement, still
        upon the tossing water, but,
        in salt transparence, at a fixed
        depth, bottom, born.

Through the museum air, the arranged light,
my procession moves towards this picture.
Our vestments, cavalcade of robes upon a dawn
horse, the moor, a camaraderie of sand
approaches, constellate: epitome
of our blurred adhesion, charge sideways.

Last night I spoke to my gift in our oblong tent:
"I reject my wisdom, but not as magic.
With its images I entertain exaltation:
the rigid star today levers my head
from the sheer path; see how I swing my arms
wide in this receptacle, how I foretell
the sky, thrusting my memories before me.

"Yet these depths will drop to their knees
before a flat tableau, among whose saints
you make your way on my behalf, edgewise,
gold apologue: 'Here, his eyes, in chains.' "

FOUR LAST POEMS

1

The poor soil around here, turned and manured for centuries,
broken down, wind and rain, and rebuilt, remains
the same poor soil. There will be no miracle crop.

Here, where the plough has sliced through
it, it holds the shape of the blade, the drenched
clay, curve and sheen of it, brief shield, brave face on it.

These pale, lined looks profile my exhaustion, yesterday.

I tramp through all the dry rooms as if

listing the ropes and flags. Nothing like life here.

I clean my nails with a dead thorn. A daffodil

catches my eye, a babble of weeds my ear. The noon

bell, drowning a bird. I land back at my bench, make up a seal

with morning in relief, set it on this place, take the

fire escape to the basement area and

there, deep in cinders, sink it.

2

"I see nothing," she said, "nothing but leaves
in a pattern. Such a future is beyond the cup's
notion of shape."

I still work, nonetheless, at these *idées fixes*,
sometimes go through with old charges
and countercharges my heart has long been
set on like a rusted-shut alarm-clock.

"A paper ship with a paper sail bears
paper Death with a paper flail, I set my
ship to cross the deep, it came
to port without the traveller,
bone, mere bone, cargo of bone."

Suddenly I am come inside this wall, through a
small door in its brick side, and where there was only face
and that shattered other faces, here is a brilliant bladder
like a blade and my arms thrown wide in it as if for
flight, and I wheeling like an upright bird and
running in place edge on in my axis, like a
mural painting knifing end first
through the tall grass around trees under the bark through
turf in rows down the boxwood hedge into the
tangle of brush, the dusky hillside itself, freeing
the new road, leaving on either side of my slicing
passage a full-face shining impenetrable evidence.

3

You've been waiting; imagine I've arrived—
never mind how—you've been waiting,
tapping your foot, and I seem not to notice
you, or how late, how long, in a blind rush
right past you almost as if running away,
not though looking back out of disgust nor
at you for fear of a direct glance or word
equally of reproach, imagine that and
how just past you I seem to run full tilt
into an invisible barricade and
am flattened (if I'd only stopped with you,
where I must have seen you, you think, too late,
blaming me) and aghast you watch me go
on, to the left, hugging the wall as if
feeling for its corner or the door through
and then still moving unchecked, still flattening,
sweep upwards in a curve vectoring
all my motions on the abrupt plane,
vining out over the masonry, hauling
myself up, tendrils in the mortar, new
shoots with astonishing speed towards some top,
some light, till I cover and am the wall,
you see its shape in my foliage, still now,
or waving in this sudden gentle wind
catching up, that of my passage or the god
of this piteous change; that is what you must
imagine, so that your foot will be still,
and that when I arrive, late as usual,
your glance, void of reproach, will receive me
not as I am but as you have lived through me
in advance, and your word open wide
its arms and your body take only
that I speed to you, stop me fast here.

Vert wrought now skewed in flight, immobile hurled, a-tremble,
still, now; bent over air into shape, thrown into rising to it,
impact, thrust leafing finding its vaumure, hinting, beyond,
the citadel, evacuated, hollow revels in echo from
now empty fields I bespeak, weasand choked, maw warm rock, back faced,
by glance of mettle from its course astonied, my waiting half
forced witness to my spilth, seeing speed wed ruin; but take me
the swerve, my use, as the wall, before an empty field, dreams.

4

        I go back, dream shapes out, mere shape as mere, more as more,
        the view held to breast till, the bout of zeal past,
        it snaps back into shape, this tone, that shapely breast
        too, out, back into sleep.
                          The eye
            in my chest heaves open,
            pneumatically, scans
            the thoracic wall.
                        What
        troth plight lights to morning?

"This knife!" she says, "I cut myself. But it din't bleed,
I watched. Just opened and pained. *Course* I wondered,
but you've got the filmiarity with anatomies and stuff."

        That's out too, plea in the flesh, *with no sensible
        diminution of the number remaining*. Then I wall up this exit.

Here's the last tale. I believe I couldn't tell it if I weren't
by now far away. Higher than ever, after the dinner, Arguth
saw rather than heard the bulbous, soutaned figures of
Père Lachaise's eloquence. How were the chiefs to be persuaded
if he was not? The priest's hand danced like a ventri-
loquist's dummy; watching it his ethylized gaze narrowed as if
caught by the token of a hypnotist, the pale, chubby hand, hung
by magic in the cavernous black stuff of its sleeve, became a
paper bird to which the priest would give flesh and then, in an
invisible flash, cause to vanish. That would move the chiefs,
if words would not. But when Arguth woke, it was the priest
who had vanished, the night had stayed, the weird chiefs,
the remains of their feast and vague palavers. One of them,
plumed and painted—was he the eldest?—came to Arguth where
he lay near the gourds and ashes: "Your shaman knows the words
of truth, like our own," he said in his dialect, "we have sent him
home to his king. Your eye"—pointing to the silver cross
on the soldier's chest—"told us you were a man of no nation,
seeking no dominion." He turned into the night as Arguth stared:
"You are free."

WALL

I

I put up, in the garden, the wall between the two spaces.

       I keep on into dark of day, straining

       to capture the original lay-out of my stones,

       addressing myself to the proper order of stones,

       knowing nothing of order until later,

       the bluff, tardy outcome, trusting my hands

       to this metamorphic rock are blood relation.

       The crystals mock, in the dusk, outcropping

       beyond the line, light corbel, all such flesh

       finery.

Dark now, the wall unfinished seems to stand
between me and any possible work.
I believe I used these very terms.

In the stone mirror is my image, caught:
that one I bury, look for authentic facing,
earth-born freestone, ready-cut cornerstone.

I look at other stones knowingly now,
building the wall up around them,
it is a glimmer: like a dawn.

I look off toward the new image over this handmade horizon.

None the less I have pictured myself in stone, as if

it were familiar prey, the way others do animals

and figures of men. My wall is the mute

in the stone trumpet, gist of me which stands,

memorial to my meaning.

Between empty lawn and empty flower bed I place
blunt monument to the stone
thrust in me, which will outlive me
as a wall without hands, without face
too, since I gave it that of stones
raised from earth and placed so
their meaning caught the light.

The stone orchestra plays my name too fast
over and over as if directed to, I
can't catch it, learn nothing unless this wall.

*This scorn to stone who works its death
in shape, as grain dies into bread,
say it's me; or as the right note struck
is slurred into the telling phrase:
the ranked flaws, clefts, crevices spell
in depth on the rock face my name,
day of birth, death-to-be, thriving.*

At night, dreaming, I walk out

to the walls, which speak of parent craft,

and find my own; on its shoulders

I lay my hands as though in blind

blessing of this low church, fatherless,

ungroined, unjoisted; dense bier.

In the dark you yield, concreted scheme which

stuck shining through the stones, you

drain off unguessed as before, and here's

the dumb pledged bulk, dry freight,

like subjects of living pain locked.

The dark wall ousts you, bulks as untold fear.

In this sense I end as stones.

II

There is the picture of the wall as I imagined it,
here's another the way it turned out,
the look identical; of what can I

brag? that the plan was drawn from life,
an artist's conception of what stood made,
trustworthy to the last visible item?

The make of it had prior claim and the wall
itself stands a judgment on its shadows;
the design it followed is mine elsewhere.

    In this ungainly perspective, the stonework

    you see finished might be anything.

    Like a marriage after the fact,

    the bulk of working trust gone, or

    the blurred wall of the child's giddy

    gaze who whirls himself dizzy in the

    park. Standing over my doings, each

    a limit of strength, I might be seeing

    a stone summer upholding a heaven

    of wattled earth; the only child of two voids;

    a *gisant*, name unknown, leading nowhere;

    a speechless compass fallen from the deadly spin.

III

one garden divide placed stone on stone stones

placed seamed face turned up over turned in hands

best face seen sought made the face last choice lost

buried in stone ground plot for stones locked fast

no pick unlocks struck down for stones for walls

elsewhere where the wall built walls in stone place

bears brunt of trowel shift's patient clumsy flaw

I withdraw into its completion as into darkness
coming on putting a stop to this work day,
pretending I'm not still over there, in the dark,
conniving at the finishing touches.

Nine. The wall trails off into voluble versions
of itself, the last thing I expected it to do.

Ten. The wall is, that when I go out to look
at it, it has none of that aura of meaning
I attach to it from elsewhere. It speaks
volumes of this fact, all one open-mouthed
word, blurted out endlessly in a chain of
images flickering by too fast to catch.
I get only the dead blur, the bleak law.

Eleven. Dragging them to light. At least in this
I gear into these uncut stones.
By exerting myself I interpret them,
this motion I bear, this wall I keep.
It is not fiction, distraction, dalliance, dream.
Nor have I made it, unless in its blatant
sense, in which it resembles me.
It is said of me that my looks offer
more than they give at first,
which is why I take such a bad picture,
and that a further promise of meaning
is made, redeemed elsewhere, but redeemed.

Midnight. All these things I say it means are
what it is, it is these things I say it is
and everything I could say it meant.
No. The wall is here, but not now; as if asleep.

Later. The stone thicker. I struggle, stop,
grind to a halt, deep in stopping,
and keep on. Pain sets between the hours.
The wall wilts, leaving the scandal.

THE WINDOW

I

The window, placed as if you could
possibly see through the wall, the glass,
reminder of common stones' weakness:
simulacrum wall, like synthetic
talk in bright palazzos, treasure-hung.

The window, which gives out, from here,
into wall, a dead window sideways,
through the thin wood frame: see-through wall
or niche for light, paradox like sand,
in museums, on which dust settles.

The window, now, framing the stone
wall inversely, outwards, the stone
held in place also by this embrasure,
considering it as shape, not weight;
or is there a weight, buttressed, into

the window, as if the stones strained
to be visible, crowding into
the picture space like the winning
team before the camera, the same
window looked through, for other reasons?

The window, by definition, locked
between lintel and sill, as the glass
between mullion and transom, escapes
these terms unnoticed in its daring
broadside presentation of light.

The window mounts this timeless drama:
the cunning sash, boxing in glazing,
would make of each pane a slice of light,
like a slide under the glass; this death
the whole window, shining, conquers.

The window, walled up from inside
with flat stones up-ended, window
into the wall, black cliff into which
you peer, the absolute difference
from self or from signs of closure.

The window sealed up, an utterly
unnatural face; stones wrenched up
on end, balanced, tottering, then
cemented in place: reverse of an
act, straight, severe window, dark cliff.

"The window, no systematist, takes in
just anything with the same glassy eye,"
such comments precisely foreign
to its whole style, oblong grip far
from slanted perspectives of artists,
     the glass so clean, so manifestly
     unbefouled, its intensity
     out of keeping with boredom, bad sleep,
     childish terror of no object,
     hash of feelings poorly received,
     hastily judged. Holding aloof,
     still, these lights transmit anything,
     smoothly, short of death, dark, paradox:
     your face behind glass, tired of looking,
     the grounds, running with children,
     the wall's bright flank hiding rubble,
     the wall stuffed into its own stiff
     shape like a sausage housing—
     anything, that is, outside them.
     The sense of fracture is our own
     wealth to renounce, anything will
     do, any window, any wall.

The window, said to open, folds
instead out of sight; air rushes
in to fill up the emptied space,
we treat with a breach of wall,
very domestic, solid pun.

The window, apparently double,
turns on its power of effacement,
the unseen, innominate bone
hinging sideways on the silent
pivot sufficient stone, wood, glass:

the window. Hurriedly opened,
the room empties into the same
precarious garden, closed in
by walls so as to open upward,
feigning an innocence of glass.
      The stained-glass light crosses
      the field of glass quickly, silently,
      without breaking anything; I know
      only because bright irrational
      movements outside, in the trees' green
      palaces, step down, coming across,
      into continuity, my kind
      of pattern: the tree, pruned by wind,
      finds at once without a break, lag
      or hesitation, stopping to think,
      and takes another form, just as
      vivid.
           Certain panes, rolled, ripple.
Others, too thick or too glossy,
is it, for standard usage,
yield bubble, stipple and pock,
limn each outline with faint spectrum
shapes leading off into unseen
blurrings, my only present guide,
through the window, possessed by light,
acting like space till my eyes close.

II

Garden ends, strictly speaking,
at the first upright surface of wall,
which, running along the garden edge,
dike to its shore, and keeping on,
means its life (the keeping on). Wall
placed and removed in a moment,
screen or partition, would leave it
a body of titles, siphon off
its brave persistence. But walls, in
several thicknesses, built up
slowly, to heights at which they become
horizon to grass at every point,
no mere boundary, found true
gardening; for eyes which see through
a fence or the vine which climbs it
make garden over into landscape,
like real property dispersed to heirs.
This is the gardener's own salvation,
his strict mandate; his garden, walled,
will not become his image, will
remain this hollyhock, flattened,
face up in the grass, this grass, this face,
these lawns, this prostrate hollow stem,
always broken, always estranged.

Otherwise the garden, end in itself
dark wall, hollow rubble and broken glass
luring worn intentions from place to place
through all the names, face to uttermost face.

You stand, outer wall, beyond the window,
beckoning me, from here, into the garden:
glass covers your teamed limbs, your heart,
pacing, its church, the whole poised flame.
A shadow view of me cuts the glare.

I reach my hand, in reply, out to
the glass horizon, depth visibly
circumscribing me, from here: my arm
measures the ground I do traverse
on the way from myself to light.
> The glass flatters, thinning out to
> the vine, the sage, hard work and care,
> gestures of mind and soil, sun and storm,
> the would-be garden, grass, garden wall:
> like a photograph of a gem. All
> views of you, even speech, give this
> flat, flat quality, unlike my hold
> on your grain, whorl, throb, true name,
> thus emphasized, a radiation,
> glass-focussed, sunshine, retarded,
> where I do not see you but catch fire.
> Our chance meeting, in the glass,
> is its form of turning point, unlike
> all those woven into days sun opens.

AN EVENING WALK, SOME YEARS LATER
I

I think this is the place.

The stream from the spring, channeled by summer children,
    following its bent, the naive line
    etched now into itself, of archaic bow
    strung, tensed brow, having called forth frowning
    of young brows over the ground of all art

Having passed, thinking this,
I turn back, walk back to look.

Having thought these things, and passed on,
turning back, I retrace my steps, to look.

The stream from the spring
lined with small stones as it was not last year.

As it was not last time I passed here
and looked. A childish masonry.

Look: this clearing, without me, might be anywhere.

II

Walking, downhill

now, the destination still fixed

in notions of return, worn smooth in my head,

of home, supper, willing hands, the village
evening, for instance yesterday,
the mountains appearing, like a black wall,
holding the recurring curve of mixed blessings.

No, but the walk shape, like

motion of steps, has its own goal, like

the printer's die destined for the page
and beyond: vicarious suffering of the fate
of plowed field unplowed, of curving
village road, broken shadows, wall and tree,
writhing in the appearance of what it takes
still to appear.

    No, but here: the road has

trailed off into unmarked meadow, barrow and brush,

into someone seeking in a sign or old

blaze or trampled run, in the sudden illusion

of depth, a way through, the face itself, turned

from you, of the innumerable superficies.

          This image
is not of our time, whose days are numbered.
But I do, I discover, live it, as it lives.
And M. Ceausescu, addressing the Party Praesidium,
lives it; and Mr. Lippmann lives it, the consummate columnist,
in ways he hasn't time, poor man, to find he can't say;
and the vocal bishop, and the distinguished critic,
and the Penguin Modern Poets—shades of the poet
who made that discovery for us,
for ourselves and our friends,
beyond the glare of publicity.

To penetrate the wood, leaving the light
of uses, custodial or lucrative,
accustom the eyes to a gratuitous dim
light: wherever the body fits will be
in its way a clearing. Though the path seems
never well marked enough for certainty
you cannot get lost; yet you cannot
avoid fearing it. You can only lose
your way, finding another. The scale map,
even when remade by aerial survey,
deals with figures and symbols and you will not
wish to be carrying it along. Heed rather
advice from the locals, remembering
they are not walkers but hunters; their hints
are winter's, or recollection's, or
too minor, or mere gossip; yet all true
to life and to the scene in their sense.
No one lifetime can obliterate a road;
the passage of time across it is visible
to the struggling sense, a scrutiny
like that of language yielding brief reward.
Where you are the land is inhabited,
and where you find no one else you must lead
on; order obtains within limits
here as everywhere while you keep to
analogy. But stop dead in your tracks,
bring your motion to a point and your walk
becomes wall fronting chaos
with a rush sideways and then stillness
trying to go on facing it,
the place become anywhere
and you, giddy, absolved of place.
But even this is a form of penetration.
Beyond the endeavor you will not go,
or else will go often. You are condemned
to form. Beyond this I cannot say.

III

I find myself out walking again.

Narrow motion across a broad front

Taking my subject from tree or stone,
quizzing the spot, to find it strength
to stand alone, to fix the find in face.

                                                Further,
by the wood, the spring glade, keeping
shadows alive within the wood. The same
spring, challenged again by art.
Moss. Gnats yaw in the breezelessness.

Already in the mouth of the path the hour
matters less.
                Wood light, a stunted dawn,
its changes changed to an inflection.
Like my own progress, as through a bowel of day.
The ground remains night under my feet.

To find my path in this waste of paths:
I think back up light to its dawning.
The unrelenting, the insidiously
undramatic dawn.
    Given morning
my feet come like light to the wall of earth.

The dubiety of my walk, step by step,

leaves no trace, the regular print assures
the ground, made to receive, by testimonial,
its self-expression.
    I fire with form
the bleak earth which holds form.

My motion, like unrisen sun, lights
a path under my feet, under guesswork.

My eyes, striking out for a grip on the sheer
vertical scene, reach air, where trees shade off
into interstellar spaces and the darkening maze
of trunks, as in deep snow.
Stuck in depth gain no further insight,

depth, like a bark to air, walling off sight
from what it has to grope for in vain.

Keeping on here, I meet no surface head on
but slip down its side, with the grain,
as if avoiding its eyes. The air, yes,
I breast, and the light, as if it were carried by it.
I am the shadow now cast in air by a stance
like mine, gait like mine, routine type of man.

I look for my face in the beech's face,

sliding up its column, its bark tube.

And it appears again, along a familiar line of sight,
that I am not the walker, not the wood;
but the shady place where the two dance
courtship, cumbrous, stately, dull.

Beyond the wood will lie the stubble field.
I can gauge, looking back, its situation,
the one it claims, legitimately, to occupy,
"the saddle wood, riding the hollow of the hill
as by right,"

        also the one forced on it,
"the wood, the evening part of the walk,
an aggravation of day, the divined uncertainty."

Across the massive wood front, nothing salient,
no part stands out, unless I, looking askance,

take this surface end on, bark literally vast.

Horizon inhabited, entasis gauged narrowly.

My gaze sweeping the trees draws from each its sound,
unmistakably, like its neighbor tree or stone
and fading. Beech tangles with mica, fir with schist.

Behind the façade, sighting down its inner curve,
its wall lining,
              I canvass the scene for signs of time.
A protruding stump, an artless tumble
of branches suggest last year, fail to quit
their place or lead out, aim to snare me into
stopping here, content with this perception.

Keeping on, against immense odds, I must find this
seeming, at last, natural. Predictable
night falls on the far side of the trees. My eyes
growing wider discount mere dimness, it is
the wood evicts me thinking dark makes me
words' fool.

Keeping on, through breakage, whole woods summed up
in the near tree. My feet feel out the last stub of path.

ALFOXTON PARK

I

The oldest possible landscape.
Meeting this. Having known,

over the days here, the hillside we climb
from every angle, setting out, to be:

>   full of illusions, like your face,
>   at first, or the projecting
>   wall, partition, you circumvent,
>   the other side naturally "the outside";
>   and we mean no less by the hill,
>   expect no less of it, this same
>   undesignated, ancient hill;
>
>   the heroic hill, its svelte body thus
>   in action, or its youth, triumphantly
>   scaling all alone the unguarded wall;
>   as if we could be the first to acclaim
>   its unexceptional beauty,
>   so continually surprising you, you
>   forget it's a wall itself, cloisonné.

Here is something in the other we can look at together.

Stick figures on a horizontal landscape,

momentarily violating this silent gravity which,

with weather, in time, brings all walls down;

us rising in its virtual dimension.

The hill, crossed by paths, diverges
from its original intent,

its shape ruined, from the top,
the way a wall, relaxing
its hold, crumbles down, the two
faces going outwards, into rubble,
moving on into what they had faced.

The hill turns, thus,

like a stone stair twisting back on itself,
feigning, while we climb, to reach upwards,
proliferating views, deep smokescreen.

To cite landscape before you: a type of reticence.

No clean breast of it could reach you half so well.

Besides, there is no other speech we'd both
    accept first, for a certainty,
    without the classic demurrer.

It is this priority I keep invoking,
    through the unutterable
    strangeness of you who share it.

In other words, this bind, your face, my love.

What, in your absence, is left of the theme
    of landscape?

like the violence of a cheap mystery,
the facts not having held up.
(With a relation *not* imaginative to his material
the story-teller has nothing whatever to do.)

From far off I reconstruct the dialogue
of departure, in my own precinct.

A study of the hill so far away it requires
a decision to climb, original leviathan,
gives rise to several interpretations;
just as the path the eyes scan reveals a paraph
scrawl, Amazonian fire scar, slash, or dull tattoo,
the something devious about it urging this
straight flight.

But the path, climbable, to the hill fort, routs
all approaches but one. I am left with the bleak hill,
underfoot, the path the eyes scan, dull tattoo,
the something unassailable behind this very English
tour de force.

Unknown continents call from the heart of here.

The hill seems to need interpreting like everything
else,
        everything being, for now, what you and I
        do not need to bend our minds to.

The hill in front of us rises like a wall:
        like the hill in a child's painting.

But in the climb, the everything else intrudes,
        like the other slope, under this, mirror
        image of the far slope, metal
        support, one and compacted of unknown,
        to this enamel voyage, eyes' passage out.

Climbing, as if with stealth, as up the side,
from our skiff, of some scaly monster
which might wake and plunge, our progress
decently concealed by its immensity,
marine Ventoux moored here for good;
and imagining, clearly, sighting down,
from the top, gained, the other side, in
changing light, the next hill, mirror image
reversed, face with paths become a wall as depth fades,
having waited for dusk to turn its back:
the face, the shifting hill, work like a sea.

Underfoot, roots, stones, dry rivulets
where the feet buy a passage, anatomy
of the wall of earth, mask the distance come
from the earlier landscape, as if
we lapped, distracted, a flat, closed field.

Vision narrows, nearing the top, sharpens
to the point of the climb, the view: pretext
and image of our setting out together.

II

Out of the wind which walks on
overhead, other summit, I stretch out
like a landscape, supported by the one
crust, of earth, in every part, and
by the other from lapsing into emptiness,
moire of images over the sheet of sky.

My locked hands in turn hold my head. Down
there, at an appalling distance,
my feet tread for once the unseen view,
      the other part, perfectly present, yet
      seemingly remote, of this ground we have
      traversed; themes and proportions support
      Exmoor and Porlock, the rocky
      coast, hills up to Dunkery, interlocked.

Pledged to notice everything, we
have observed nothing definitive so far:
a motion of two related vitalities,
like seining dories, dragging the ground,
delight, constraining to rest, and vigilance,
holding up our end as we conceive it;
the considered tone of speech which arises
where we stop, trained on absent consequences,
reweaving in a larger frame the curt
queries, baptisms, espousals of the climb,
my accurate verve, your pure diffidence,
abashed responses to the unnerving;
more or less familiar feelings, relished
on that scale, if remarked, moving us on another
with their own drift, and, always shoaling,
that waste of feeling where the familiar floats.

These are definite shapes, if blurred in passing.

The other, for each, names them once and for all.

"Yesterday we sat, like this, down
by the stream, staring across it,
overhearing its babble at
this point, by the praying alder.
An invisible line, you said,
ferried our gaze to the farther
bank and back, sectioning its change.
You said this was its flux, for us,
the crosswise stream I was perplexed.

"I have trouble following too
your vision of high seas among
scorched furze and bracken-bare hilltops.
As if we were in no season.
Behind us as we clomb today
was the sea, a shore we could hear,
the green plain meeting wood and hill.
Such clarity confirms our own
presence here, visible intent.
Yet your words light up my portion
of our landscape; so that I hang,
in a more than literal sense,
on each, cling to our passage as,
in our talk, I cleave to your theme:
live objects. Oh, were you myself,
where would I find sanction for hope?

"This is as close as I can get:
I have tried to hold to this thought,
that all we say to each other
wells up at the place where we meet,
within our bond, a turn of mood,
fills a need while we pace along;
that not one phrase should be allowed
to stand aloof, in judgment on
the speaker, final, absolute,
lifeless, binding. This comforts me.

"I have my journals, stopgap, shorthand.
I mention none of this there. I have told
Coleridge so. I do not keep his letters."

CRUST AND KEY

I. *Crust*

Hill. The hill, always this hill, fixed.

From which, on its side, one with it:
views.
        The village, coming back, in a new light.
Like being up on a ladder.

New light. This stretch of pasture,
a reach of road innocent of me.

Not the tree, in a fury, torn up by the roots,
the torn roots, not this extreme, viewed from here.
Not this helpless extreme.

    The blade without true temper
    still cuts, will sharpen,
    to a degree.
           A clear view, for a
    moment, striking home.

    The village, dangling by my eyes from the hillside,
    elsewhere rooted in hills and undenied.

Well. Pattern within pattern, like numbers,
   number within numbers.

Like the well: to be drawn from,
   speaking within speech.

Dark from dark, water from water, at
   water level: this frequent core.

Or the line of hills: hills, hills, hills,

         viewed, say, from the lookout,
         where you follow the campaign
         through the paying telescope
         a coin opens and locks, ticking:
         the line of hills, brief close-up,
         framing embattled distance,
         the long tube you sight down
         optically flattens; shuts.

   Coming down the hill the mind leaps home:

   like a foreign language, "shortcut to success,"

   or the sloping street, paving the way home,

   like wheels, from the store: wheels and packaged goods,

   necessary accessories, wheeling, mind, home,

   and "How do you like my accessories?"

How can you draw a hill without lines

(the awkward shading where no shade is)?

The hill folded, like looking through

        a telescope sideways; or a bundle
        of Sunday newspapers, the paper wall.

The line, always the line shows the hill crest,
    not the hill, say, cresting.

Where there is a line you can draw one,

elsewhere, bundles of lines, insincere,
giggle, renege illusion, the line of tradition,
one whole draughtsmanship, line up
kicking like a bunch of chorus girls,
the leggy ensemble, working at it.

Those are trees, perhaps, their massive
motion, brown quarry; what you see
surfaces from the page like bark from tree
trunks, sideways, towards you,
doing without lines, casting no shadow.

Uncomprehendingly webbed feet climb
   over the hill.
Climb over the ground, shadowing

it, briefly, then meet it, dark.

        At extreme range my volar glance,
        setting down, leaves out nothing,
        nothing: every detail is there,
        even unseen, as if underfoot.

My eyes run their hands over the

hill's closed features, dear vis-à-vis,

condemned window, one solid braille.

I make my largest guess, the hill
    altogether ornithoid:
      too proud to fly, like those birds,
      wingless, their meaning atrophied.

I hang every sight on this thread,
    my own motion, the line I take
    with the hill, countering its threat.

No need to enumerate.
The whole hill warrants each beauty its place.
We know all this.
You cannot hang your life on a hill.

II. *Key*

What is the story behind that scar?

What first surface, faced with flaming
    tissue now, first suffered breach?

What wound, masked by the proud flesh,
    holds in its line the clue?

I walk my eyes over the hill, searchingly.

Webbed feet, as of a bird, clamber
    over its steppes, the slippery grass,
    the crusted soil, the rock scars,
    the rigid unmapped intensity.

Shrieks of an unknown bird, the
    rush of wind, the plodding
    assimilation, wet feet to cold clay,
    give material for a legend.

Story and map, song and motion, the hill,
    clumsily healed where ploughs passed,
    offers endless beauties to be called
    forth, trophies to my rout, the healing forms.

The key hill. Which opens the whole chain
of hills; almost like a military position.

> (The hill, caught in a wind of light,
> staggers; clouds move, the hill
> shrinks back, retreats from exposure.)

Act and thought turn on its dictates,
inveigling you like love, logic, style.

> (The key grates in the lock, having
> entered its void, forest of
> polished parts, brass, oilless.)

The hill's indefinite extent, underfoot,
wars with its fixed pose, madonna-and-child.

> (The innumerable stories masking
> the story line, as in the folded papers,
> or Cocteau's pin pushed through the bunched cloak.)

This question of a story . . .

The fleshy lock: how will a key not fit?

I am like the man you carefully entrusted
with the whole bunch of keys and who then
finds every door in the damned house standing
wide open.

I move out into the landscape, struggle,
lock and return, like the key which jams.

I walk out, look left and right
as if at a dangerous crossing.

I walk out, look right, left, first, sight
blocked off blind by green cataracts,
a crust of earth sealing up my eyes
like stucco keyed to stone, condemned wall,
my bit of hill. The hillside, one green shade,
the details locked in place, equivalent
of a musclebound imagination,
of a facile, fertile imagination.
Too close-set to enumerate.
Beneath the escharous tissue,
under the reddened boughs, swollen leaves
and tumid meadow: like a peatbog,
hints of a dark deed, dressing of a wound.

Seeing nothing at a dangerous
crossing, seeing too much: field traffic.

I walked out that spring morning after mushrooms,
though there were none in sight, my vigorous strides
betokening destinations of their own.
I went over the ground carefully, where
the mushrooms were, or could be thought to be,
the pure, white shapes in their rings, edible,
feeling much more like the Leech-gatherer
than like his wondering interlocutor.
There was nothing in the grass; which took my
whole gaze, fixed as if in prayer; and I met
no one at all, yet I was not stymied,
or vexed, while the hillside filled my vision,
until I lost myself, the walk, the day,
in this renewed green adventure.
Above the grass my formal thoughts returned
and traced their healing patterns; of the man,
the well, the lock, its core and wards, the hill;
the hill, its dark flagitious tale, unread,
my vision, strangely palmiped.
I thought of others out of key with their
lives, the great cities, their walls and exiles:
Parmenides, fighting all appearance,
and Keats dying, blind with surfeit and loss;
the aged Bach, and Milton, dictating,
his Samson, Homer, and the Theban king
who opened his eyes with a gold pin.
"No one has stood, whole, on the bleeding earth.
One man, one hill suffice to riddle a universe."

DECEMBER

I

To stir, the surface shivering, bulging
faintly, like a becalmed sail at first wind,
a scarcely visible, local ripple,
hesitant increase of tautness as if,
tarp stretched over a cargo of barely
elastic substance it could stretch tighter
only by thinning, like a balloon skin,
revealing an inner shape and the new
force swelling it out from slackness to self
expression, to gather itself as if
to spring, with mechanical suddenness
to lift clear of a floor where it had seemed
to stand imperturbable and rise,
transformed, stiff beige drill slung on ropes and yard,
with a faint tuneless squealing of tackle
like a backdrop wound up into the loft
leaving you face to face at once, shiftless,
with a widening oblong of scuffed boards
and dull horizonless cyclorama:

this is what the whole wall, window
in it and outside refuse to do.

Or to crumble, like an upright puzzle,
jig-saw pieces you spread on the table;
or to light in an artificial shape,
none the less its own, shown in crisscross
lines, like the solemn evergreen as you
tested the switch last evening, on and off,
the purchased tree, awkward there, vanishing;
or the sacred print, caught in the fire you
were fearing, flames sweeping up the wall from
the shorted socket, fake snow as tinder,
the glass shattered, the frame shattered and charred,
and the straw flaring, the ancient structure,
in that brutal dawn, crumpling, the figures
too, the coarse and the superb onlookers,
and the crèche, on the fragile paper the
infinite ink, crushed by the hand of flame:

the hill, raked by the hand of winter,
leaves swept away, crops reaped and stored.
resists such temptations, "to
cave in like a dry toothless cheek or
open its harrowed side and belch flame";
the house stands clear of encumbering
vines, slow shadow of trees nearby,
hand of the summer cloud's flight
to façades, stands fast, stammering.

Neither to sink, the hill, with pathetic
gurgles, like an overturned hull, stove in,
nor liquefying, going all jelly,
to slide down into its trough, our valley,
the unaccountable inundation,
unheralded by rains, rising water,
the wall of water swallowing the house,
balked walls, floors, windows, crushed like an eggshell:

these missing, catastrophic visions
the hillside, which I descend, suggests,
and will not, will not embody,
byproduct of its workings in
and out of season, restless,
the way a ship "works" in a heavy sea,
or faces, from shore, watching it go down;
suggests at its limits, extra
fringe above the trees as it moves through the clouds,
aureole bonding it to these,
of sky, or comet's tail, streaming
banner of blood; the hill itself,
studied, melts into images
of ripped soil, ripped, seeded, frozen shut,
over-grazed grass, ground elbowing through,
high tattered façade, rough stucco,
mortar of dirt and lime, over stones,
"uninhabitable house, inside out,
simple wall in the hands of the tenth month";
here, at one, its burden and wreck.

To slough its whole visible coat, pasture,
tree-fringe and plowland splitting, rumpling down,
revealing the carcass, gray cone of slag
which bursts like Mt. Pelé on the houses
of Saint-Pierre, leaving one survivor:

these threats it brandishes, the hill,
the fragile road I take, going down,
which first cold rains bring to ruin,
the thicket, vacated, tumble-down;
these strings attach to the hill's most
solid clause, on either hand its
smooth wealth escheats before I
can renounce or squander it; this
is its subtle bluster, its just
noticeable swagger, working
hypothesis supplanted just as
the question of its truth is raised;
the hill, no thinker or doer, stands
there, proposing a climb, motion pushed
up to the hill wall, hill lethal
to fancy and every known
faculty, unbinding the will;
colors can fade out, stubble freeze,
under the first disfiguring
snow the rise and fall of its lines,
fence and pasture by the ruined road,
spells out its terms, final exits.

II

Funny. I trudge off on my rounds, it isn't
    exactly me who disappears, but an outbound
    variant of the man you know.
Everyone has like his own little language,
    a technical jargon pretty much beyond you,
    the text of his bargain with life.
    Maybe that isn't so funny after all.
Golf or mineralogy or the locksmith's lingo,
    what you need's not a glossary
    A to Z, but a set of clear pictures.
Mr. Vholes, for example, with his "buttoned-up voice"
    and "smoke-dried face," whose business was
    "making hay of the grass which is flesh."
Temporarily baffling, "wealth" which "escheats,"
    "catastrophic visions," and "the hill,"
    "the besetting sin, comma, of paths, comma,
    being, comma, to peter out, dot dot dot."
I enter the baby-clothes shop and ask for
    a fire extinguisher, her husband's line,
    she queries, gentle, "What's the firm?"
What is weymann the clerk says his first car was made of?
    What's ashlar and parpen under the mason's hand?
    scrim, drop, batten in the set-designer's ear?
"Booth-ey! Hey Boothey, give us an analogy!"
    BARUCHH. "The sound you just heard is Boothey's brains
    being blown out by an enemy shell.
    Come into the house and shut that door!"
One silence will blot them all out and it won't be
    silence of my making, so will my
    voice remain, my name in a white stone?

Last beasts lick the freezing turf,
liverwort, dandelion, cress,
flat colors the snow will blot out;
the ground, sloping, carries me back,
descending the hill, by the road,
towards the house; I imagine,
even while it comes into view,
the stone cube, hollow, rival hill,
the back wall, the room behind it,
the window where you think I sit,
balked by glass, arris and reveals,
bright sky like a page of depth
opened on my table top:
this marrying of images
is the mystery I profane
naming its secrets abroad in
dense terms, useless forms, the year's
impenetrable liturgy.

September. Under the shelled hill, by the
burning farm house, the Emperor got down,
his head pounding from the heat and the pain.
He hobbled to a nearby stump and sat.
Using his hat as support he scribbled:
"To die leading my troops into battle:
failing even at this, what can I do
but place my sword in Your Majesty's hands?"
"These words," he thought, "will put an end to it."

Before the Hill

HILLSIDE

The King holds all the trumps! some such

announcement, stiffening the air,
rolls, beats, lines and sizes the air.

I set this canvas like a sail.

    Moving, laterally, across the hillside:

        over the hillside, close up, a new slant,
        one foot of necessity higher,
        exactly as if you were climbing.

    The hillside, like a grassy beach:

        the stream, below, running
        sideways, making a shore,
        liquid commissure, dry extent.

The air, meanwhile, or something
like it, wedge-shaped, invests these solids

as if resounding: timpani, sennet,
and banners streaming, procession of air.

Liquid commissure, dry extent,
the valley, wedge or keel of air:

think of the traveling we did to get here.

      Bow meeting the perfectly calm
      sea, worked into waves by wind and
      wind over miles of ocean.

      Atlantic skuas, or plovers,
      wheeling, with cries, about the ship:
      obsessed by currents of air, by flight,
      the truly light, fluid element,
      slaves to it, owned, pinioned there,
      an obtrusive, ventilated sphere.

      And Mallarmé, below deck, seasick, not
      quite making roll and pitch rime with language:
      "Foreign lands, it's nonsense. Islands and so forth
      Conversation pieces for sea between."

But the rocky shore, arriving, grass and
rock-strewn slope, where keel ground:

scorched zone, banked road, like a front line;
upwards trench, defeating sea sideways.

The hill, refractory, resists
the foot: I inculcate nothing,
this its support, my assurance.

Borne on this swell of pasture I remain:
this noble individual, crossing,
register of its repeated extents;

> thinking, life isn't home, truth isn't elsewhere;
> but you are not exactly here, despite the travel.
> How long has it been since we arrived?
> as if you were waiting, beforehand,
> at a tryst, say, or rendezvous:
> and the other is moving towards you,
> loping, breathless, or flagging a taxi,
> hurrying the driver, the museum
> an agony of rain and traffic away,
> thinking, lover rimes with suffer, anguish
> invests these solitudes with a resounding wish.
> Still, you arrive, in a second it's over.

Something stark, ungarnished about
such extent, thick with its own
uneven growth, like a legal writ.

You look in your way, find in your image.

I have lost track of what there is to
see, and flight, the fluid element.

But the hill, as stark as you like . . .

But hillside, sheer extent, vast detail,
defeats any strict accounting.

The adequate hill? brick-and-mortar hill?
law-abiding hill? you can't reason with it,
any more than with the body of common law.
The bourgeois hill? you can't tamper with it

      either: its terrain uneven, from the proper
      distance, walking, upright, on, or over
      it, necessary declivities;
      close up or from across the valley:
      smooth as butter, denuded, all one.

      The way the past smooths out as you
      leave it, tide-washed sand, someone's
      footsteps effaced gradually, sideways.

Here all skills go begging.

Still, it seems you can proceed, over
      the banked sand, through the resounding air.

You can leave the pasture, suddenly, where it ends,

entering the wood: the thin gray wood,
coppiced hornbeam, hazel and ash, its edge
almost, not quite, the edge of life, by
a syllable, a word, the bark of a tree:
article of awareness, skin of your teeth.

Or again, in the middle of the field,
stop short, before the tree, reigning alone
here, left the cattle for shade torrid days,
this tree, this shaded realm, good use made of it;

and once you've got a tree you've got forest.

Or, by an effort of imagination out of doors,
enter the past, the hill as it must
originally have felt to someone lost
on it: forested slope, leading down or up.

Or at last, pulling yourself together,
before the hillside, even before the
one tree, face the predicament squarely,
here, backed by these expressions of it
you will have tried to put behind you.

Elsewhere: you move here from elsewhere,
to these employments, guarded, tense, somewhat
like the tree whose core, sheathed in usual regalia,
in visible bark, flowering fountain of leaves,
takes the sun here; bends to every wind.

What are we to make of it, the tree
you're only somewhat like? this fixed extent
you cross walking to meet this passionate
encounter? Where are you before you start?
for you do, sitting there, have it in mind:

the tree, not exactly measurable,
fulfilling any image, every
discardable image, but one.

THE *CHEVREFOIL* OF MARIE DE FRANCE

from the Twelfth-Century Anglo-Norman

Yes it's my idea, to tell you
just the very nub of the tale,
the adventure called Chevrefoil:
how and why it came down to us,
as I have put it together
from a dozen sources, the whole
bundle of choppy episodes,
some of them written up, the best,
but everyone's got his favorite.
The tale of Tristram and the Queen:

high love; long pain; then tragic death.

A dozen witnesses at most.

Not counting the king; yet the whole
kingdom knew, the word got around,
an acknowledged incoherence,
nub, episodes, the whole story
hung by what thread? it's hard to say.

Mark the King, his anger; anger
borne by his own nephew Tristram,
the earnest, the skilled, the devout;
whom he's sent away from the realm,
sent back to South Wales, his birthplace.

For her sake, whom he loved, the Queen!

The whole year he bore it at home,
going through the motions at home.
Then threw it up, no turning back,
gave himself to death and ruin.

When you're in love body and soul
and you can't have your way, you turn
wretched, vexed; tormented, scheming:
no, nothing unnatural there.

Tristram's wretched; distraught, absent.
So he leaves home without thinking,
making a beeline for where, in
that far stretch to Land's End, Cornwall,
he knew she was staying, the Queen!

Loping on foot, over the bare
Quantock Hills, Exmoor, Dartmoor, to

the forest: he thrust on, alone,
and guideless, no one should see him,
only emerging at evening,
the end of the endless June day,
when it was time to find lodging.

Humble peasants he asked at dusk
for shelter and news: of the king,
for instance, what was he up to?
Everyone goes to Tintagel!
The King has sent for all his men,
festivities for Pentecost,
that's the story; with them the Queen!

Tongues of fire, first-fruits of spirit.

Tristram hears it, the mood changes.
As she travels he'll see her pass.
The day she sets out their paths cross.
The day! and the court's in motion.

Tristram, back, the dim forest, eyes
used to it now, reaches the long
forest track king and court must take:
still, empty, perpendicular.

A tree, hazel, sapling, sturdy:
he hacks it in two, squares it up,
skillfully cleans the stem with his
knife, and with his knife writes his name;
signs his name to the hazel staff.

If the Queen keeps her eyes open,
usually she's on the lookout,
since already it had happened
this way, she'd glimpsed a sign this way,
she'll know whose handicraft it is,
seeing the articulate tree;
what tree it is, seeing his work.

       The rest of it you know: the Queen . .
       how the Queen . . . you know already.

Such was the gist of the message
he had spelled out that early time,
when the words flowed you could cherish,
each tale took embroidering on:
how he had waited and waited;
biding his time in the forest;
and hoping some plan would emerge,
and hoping to learn of his chance
to see her, to see her, the Queen!
for he could not live without her.

Their union was as close as that,
as honeysuckle and hazel,
the one so twined and tight clinging
about the stem which supports it,
mutually they stand, locked to life;
try to undo the bond, they say,
try unlacing the knotted tree,
the tree dies, and the vine follows.
"Sweet, here's our way, apart, together:
one does not live without the other."

Here she comes, riding by, the Queen!
keeping a lookout the whole time.
The hazel staff! she picks it out.
She reads each letter of its name.
Thinking quickly, her armed escort
about her, she orders a halt;
she wanted to get down and rest
a bit, here in the cool forest.
The cavalcade stops short, perplexed.

In that crew no one she can trust.

Brenguine has proved loyal, her maid .

Calling her she steps out bravely
at right angles to the roadway;
beyond the first trees and into
the forest, where she finds, hidden,
someone who loves her more than life.

Here was a private festival!

There was room to converse freely.

She could say what was on her mind:
how to regain the King's good will;
her distress at his banishment;
the King had acted thoughtlessly,
deceived by jealous whisperings . . .

These points made she got up to go,
yet parting was not so easy.
They faced being cut off again:
the strain on them both told in tears.

Back to Wales went Tristram to wait
until his uncle sent for him.
By then he had made the story
into a piece of poetry,
set to music, sung to the harp,
beautifully, by Tristram himself.

It expressed the joy he had found
in his loved one, the sight of her;
and at the Queen's own suggestion
told of the message he had sent
in those memorable phrases.

Here's the pithy name of the piece:
Gotëlef's the English version,
while the French call it *Chevrefoil*.
That's the true story behind it,
this tale which I've just recounted.

TERRAIN

Here is the place the Queen must pass.

Understand this whole part takes place
on the hillside as it once was:
forested, densely, dark with trees;
boasting a solid vertical
dimension of murk and branches.

        An inhabitable bulkhead—
        or wall—between the ground and sky.

        Apparently eloquent. Dark
        pitch, dizzying, predicament.

The wooded slope; rather the slope
of wood. How long have we been here?
endless likely answers occur.
Our wine was mixed for a known span,
our time keyed to a foreign past.

Sense of, somewhere, proper order,
fresh clothes, bread and milk: touch and go
in this front line. Wilderness. Damp.
The hunt without ceremony.
No two nights touching the same ground.

        Penury.
        Tremendous reconciliation.
        Feigning tremendous reconciliation.

Whoever fixed the loving cup
built in such ordeal. Plus dread:
of a fiercer outside its walls.
Peace would call for double treacle,
another science, second cup.

One fierce draught has made us outlaws,
locked the courteous dimension.
Plausible courage makes this fate
steps taken, each day, into a loose
pocket of pain, durance, drama.

Depth comes closing around us now:
a fixed reach of small light, then death;
light sailing among the farthest
trees, wrecked on the leafy shallows,
the bark coast, Cornwall, the forest.

       Yet the Queen will, she will

       emerge behind apparent trees . . .

       I get this idea from the tree.

       Some madness does sustain us, thus
       far, this way; an edge-on purpose,
       taxing our strength on purpose.

I don't see how a man could get it into his head,
the half of what we went through then: if so,
and we forget, as people do, who will ever know?

True forest fixes your wandering
urge, its gravity overawes
every civilized investment.
We have what we have: the having
forfeit, on that understanding.

You cannot call us scavengers.
We are not ailing; this is no
junket. Hemlock, hazel, birch, beach
lend their names to the proper growth:
our own name our own adventures.

No sentiment either. But headlong
indulgence in trivial heroisms.

Behind best behavior: turmoil.
Like another jurisdiction.
Like the foil backing a mirror.
Like the true forest, still around,
somewhere, backing up our story.

                    Here all
        skills go begging. What tongue explores
        the least-confessed branch of passion?

The King holds the trumps, finally.
I can only taunt with the truth
my accusers, safe in one of
my foolproof disguises, schooled in
safety in equivocation.

                But where in this equivocation . . .
                where . . . in this one-sided version
                of equivocation . . .

Sweet, here's our way, apart, together:
one does not live without the other.
Like surface and depth, current-torn;
forest trail marking forest floor,
or flame, tearing free of firewood.

Or take this privileged emblem,
discarding the whole wooded slope,
the forefront of its evidence,
the poetry writ large: take this
one tree, the tree in poetry.

        But where, in this present distress,
        radiating out like depth . . .
        where . . .

        High love, which we have no words for,
        but images, images of . . .

But where, in this present absorption,
went good and evil? The King's head,
full of infidelities, treason,
guile proven on us by ordeal:
and what gave Marie the idea?

                Does reading a tree make history?
                Is self-knowledge a diagnosis?

Of all my names, which best spells out
this emergency? Should I say:
our sickness means that we prefer
our sickness to the frightful cure?
Is what we're doing abhorrent?

                Should I find, in this lofty tale,
              a culprit? a villain? a meaning,
              like a petty larceny, both
              curiously in and out of place,
              like a corkscrew in a hospital?

              Adultery? incestuous?

A forest theodicy?

Where was I that day?
What is my alibi?

Crime comes down to this persuasive
edge, slashing the true tree, carving
in wood a banished name, slicing
to no avowable purpose,
noble cause, silk joy, derring-do.

Where is the story you'd follow
in this wood? a bewilderment.
Has this happened before? once? twice?
Still, the face of those few letters,
pale gleam, page light, lure and beacon.

This dull knife will cut through the bark
to a fixed depth only, of bark,
to the white sap-drenched wood, once-dark,
sap-slippery, revealing its
blank page look only where I cut

the letters of one of my names,
eye-white within the lettering,
the wooden slope, rather the slope
of wood, sporting brachylogies,
here is the place the Queen must pass.

To block out plans, half-consciously;
to use simple craft on ready
materials, a powerful hand;
to see it through, get the results
imagined, brief, equivocal:

with blanched face, torn clothes, bleeding bowels,
to let the light through between sharp
trumeaux, dead windows, flat forest,
tryst of a few words, repeated,
expedient we're driven to . . .

     . . . meeting place.

     Words at hand . . .

Words at hand; whatever I do
I end up naming penalties:
of speech and its awarenesses.
As if caught up despite myself
in the last hearings of a suit.

        Or like the navigator lost
        in trigonometry.

        Seas rising, small craft warnings.

        I must have something spontaneous ready
        when the Queen comes riding through the woods!

Fanciers of fine points, rich fare,
will cook up our inner debates.
Surviving pain, accepting joy,
seeing clear in this tangled brew
have left us no scruples to spare.

These are the rituals of speech.
To be caught up despite yourself
in its liturgy, handed down
from another age, feasting on
the age-old, desuete distinctions.

"This incident recalled my mind
 to its old track: there seemed to be,
 here, the groundwork of a tale . . ."

The dream farm, elsewhere; health, death, shared;
inner England, among Alps, too
high to climb; your story a song
of verse by firelight, the timeless
adventure, accurate romance.

"Beroul on board, not speaking to Thomas;
 Eilhart, Gottfried; Wagner, supercargo;
 and Mallarmé, below deck . . ."

"We can't speak without using words
 as if they had meaning, as if their meaning
 were fixed and as if it were our meaning.
 But our meaning is never fixed, beyond
 a certain depth, is always emerging."

The white wood wall, naming itself;
the silent forest, drunk on trees;
terrain without arbitrament,
lacking art yet wasting no time:
perpetual emergency.

Terrain denuded, whatever
you might think, depending on how
you read it, "terrain," "denuded";
yet the Queen will, she will emerge,
upright, lithe, golden, odorous.

        like dancing water,
        like the surface of sundancing
        water when it sprays and
        splashes and refreshes and
        laughs outright, dancing
        before the eyes and down the throat.

        An amusing woman . . .

        From behind the trees,
        polite laughter, crude song, in
        snatches, horses and cloaks,
        her cavalcade, the Queen!

TREE

The chance tree? the key tree? opening the field?

Asking: Will you know how to read me right?
Who's to say I put words where they don't go?

The unerring tree? leading me deeper in?

A preponderance of tree, squeezing me out?

Stepping back, keeping your distance, you could be
shooting the tree, in its hillside set-up,
its stance on light, the black and white hillside.

Or you could be in the tree:

                    braced,

picking its fruit or pruning dead branches;
holing up with sardines in its house, waiting to fall on
an enemy horseman, overhear blackguards conspire;
or have wrenched its scabby, barren stick from its socket;
or dug your hand into its rotting heart,
surgeon, or gardener, seeking humus, and "mulch."

        The adventitious tree? the tree we're fortunate in?
        the way we are in Shakespeare, in Pasteur?
        Dwight Eisenhower, Ralph Nader, Buster
        Keaton? or in each other?

        The staunch tree? genuine article?
        top sergeant, foster-parent, hard as nails?

        The cossetted tree? the proverbial
        pet lamb? favorite pilgrimage,
        written up from every angle? text?

The vaunted tree? Calling its bluff.

But with its connivance, under its aegis?
a vehement partnership? or a vicious needling?

Dear tree. Deep tree. The tree sponsoring you,
encouraging you to read your own thoughts,
helping you to put your words on the table:

wall, road, window; hill; hillside, table.

The English tree, or the French tree?

The trenchant tree, rooted tree, invisible tree.
Making a clean sweep of thoughts and words.

The showdown tree, provoking emergencies?
In your mind its word is law:
canon, martial, maritime law? Lynch law?

The wild tree? unpruned, unshriven?
mutilated by neglect? or by crude hands?

The English tree or the French tree.
The tree in the state of nature: the pure tree,
against the gold dawn, all tree.

The bitter tree? the blinding tree?
or the blinding cloud it's in?

The stony tree? the wooden tree?

The tree ad-libbing:
stone tree, cork tree, fruit tree, dead tree, thus
the tree rehabilitating itself.

The voracious tree, raking in your pittance.

Installing its own courts, its own terms,
like a Norman conqueror.

The native tree, there before you.

The arduous tree? the tree swept and garnished.

The cloying tree. The loathsome tree.

The triumphant tree, at its foot a Queen.

PRINCETON SERIES
OF CONTEMPORARY POETS

Returning Your Call, by Leonard Nathan
Sadness And Happiness, by Robert Pinsky
Burn Down the Icons, by Grace Schulman
Reservations, by James Richardson
The Double Witness, by Ben Belitt
Night Talk and Other Poems, by Richard Pevear
Listeners at the Breathing Place, by Gary Miranda
The Power to Change Geography, by Diana Ó Hehir
An Explanation of America, by Robert Pinsky
Signs and Wonders, by Carl Dennis
Walking Four Ways in the Wind, by John Allman
Hybrids of Plants and of Ghosts, by Jorie Graham
Movable Islands, by Debora Greger
Yellow Stars and Ice, by Susan Stewart
The Expectations of Light, by Pattiann Rogers
A Woman Under the Surface, by Alicia Ostriker
Visiting Rites, by Phyllis Janowitz
An Apology for Loving the Old Hymns, by Jordan Smith
Erosion, by Jorie Graham
Grace Period, by Gary Miranda
In the Absence of Horses, by Vicki Hearne
Whinny Moor Crossing, by Judith Moffett
The Late Wisconsin Spring, by John Koethe
A Drink at the Mirage, by Michael J. Rosen
Blessing, by Christopher Jane Corkery
The New World, by Frederick Turner
And, by Debora Greger
The Tradition, by A. F. Moritz
An Alternative to Speech, by David Lehman
Before Recollection, by Ann Lauterbach
Armenian Papers: Poems 1954-1984, by Harry Mathews
Selected Poems of Jay Wright, edited by Robert B. Stepto,
Afterword by Harold Bloom

Library of Congress Cataloging-in-Publication Data

Mus, David, 1936-
WALL TO WALL SPEAKS / David Mus.
p. cm.—(Princeton series of contemporary poets)
ISBN 0-691-06728-7 (alk. paper)   ISBN 0-691-01444-2 (pbk.)
I. Title. II. Series.
PS3563.U8337W3 1988   87-29200
811'.54—dc19

GPSR Authorized Representative: Easy Access System Europe - Mustamäe tee
50, 10621 Tallinn, Estonia, gpsr.requests@easproject.com

www.ingramcontent.com/pod-product-compliance
Lightning Source LLC
Chambersburg PA
CBHW081422230426
43668CB00016B/2324